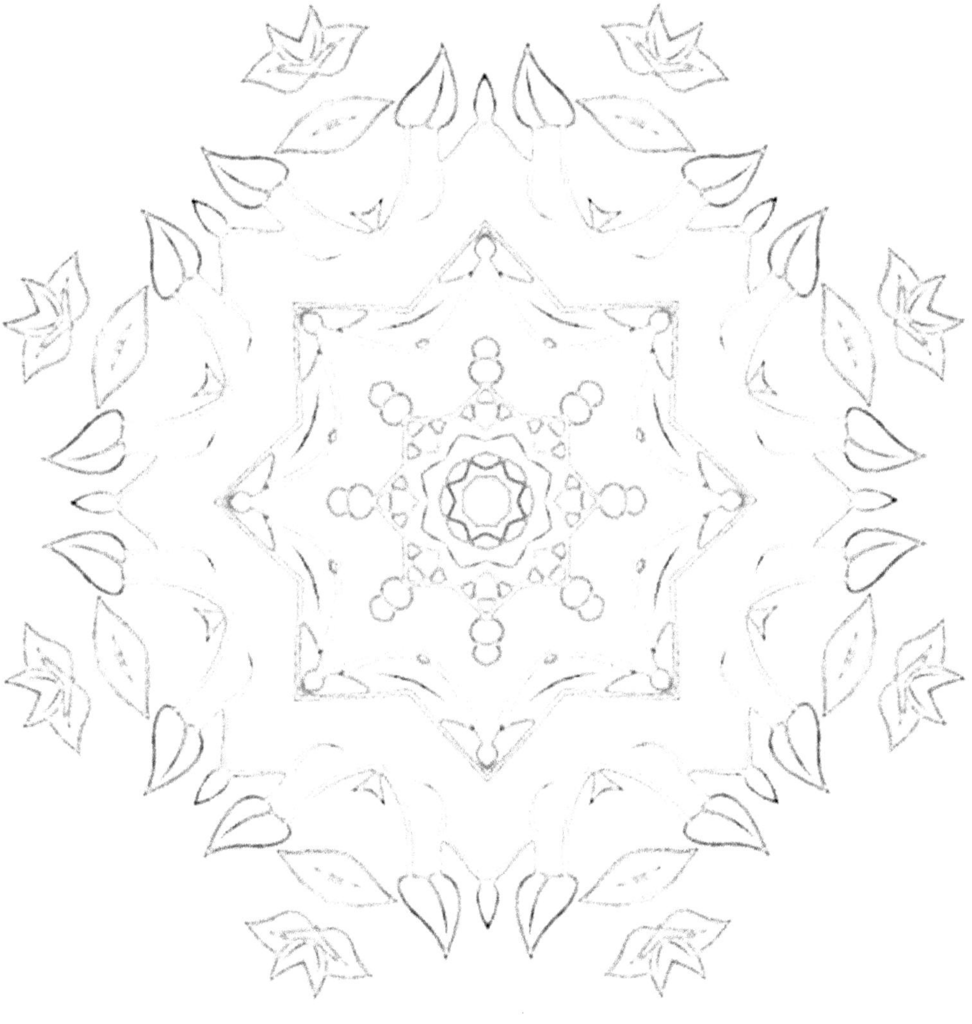

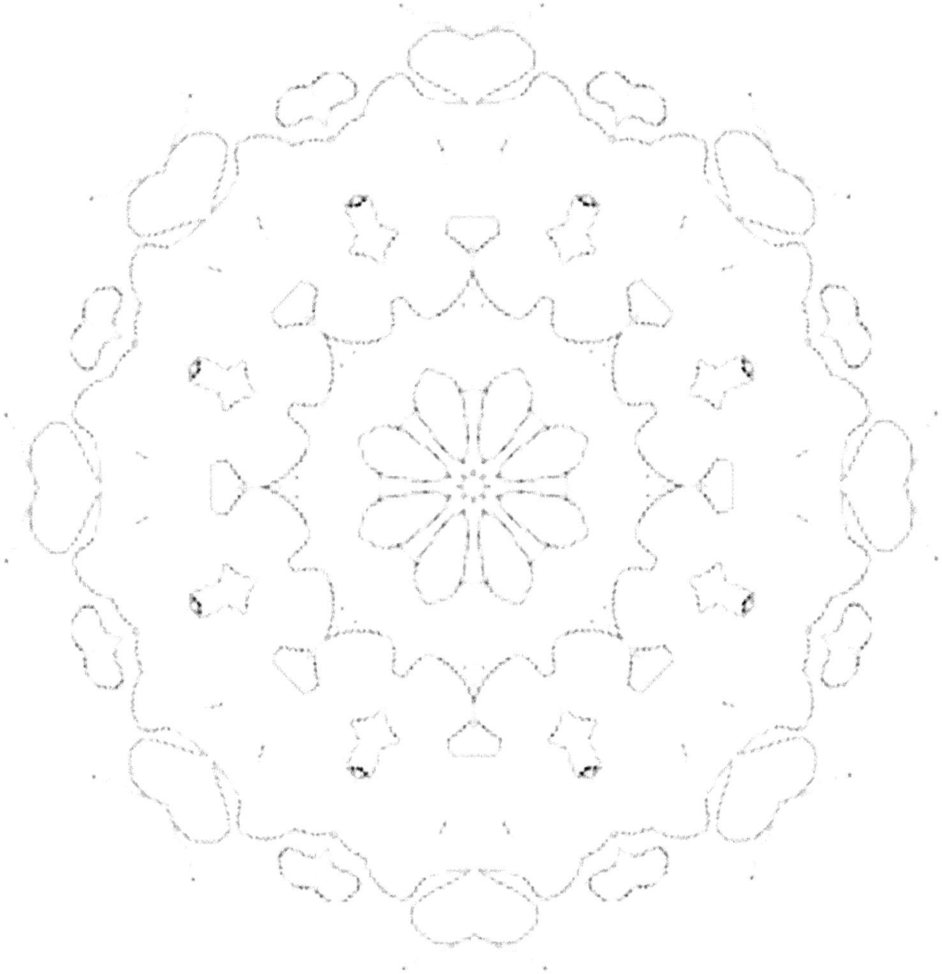

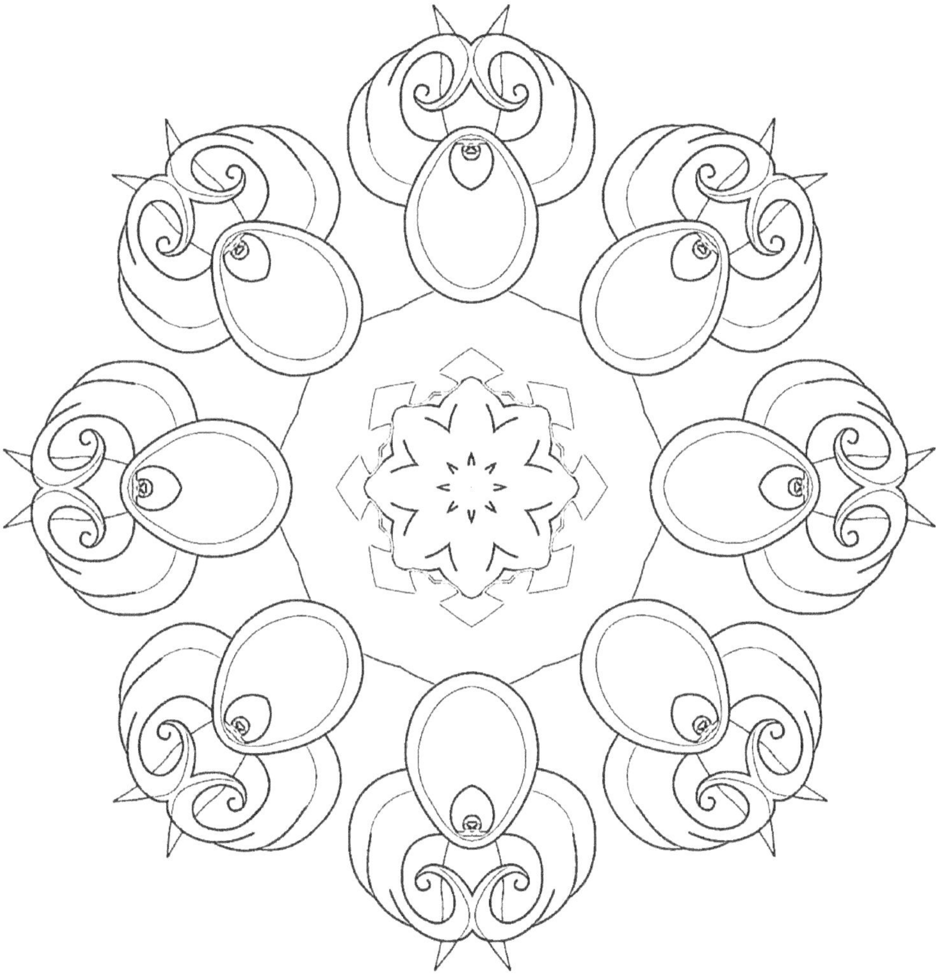

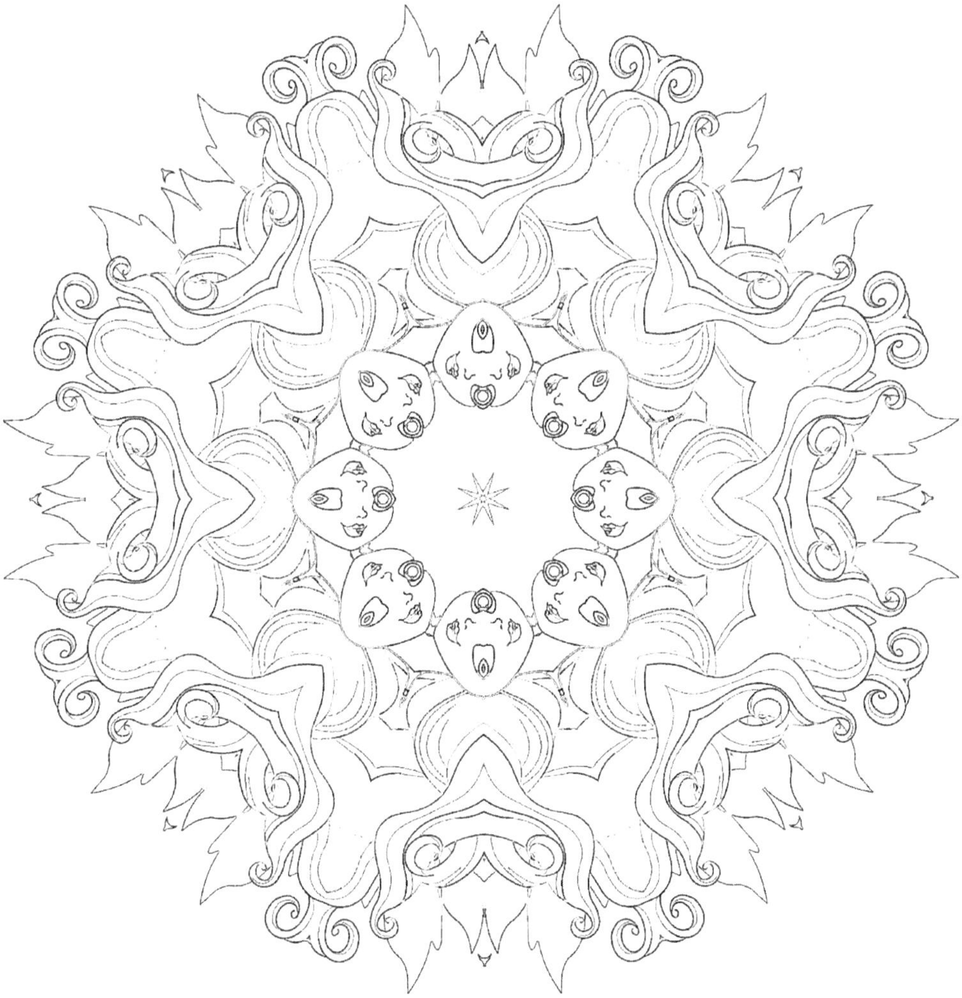

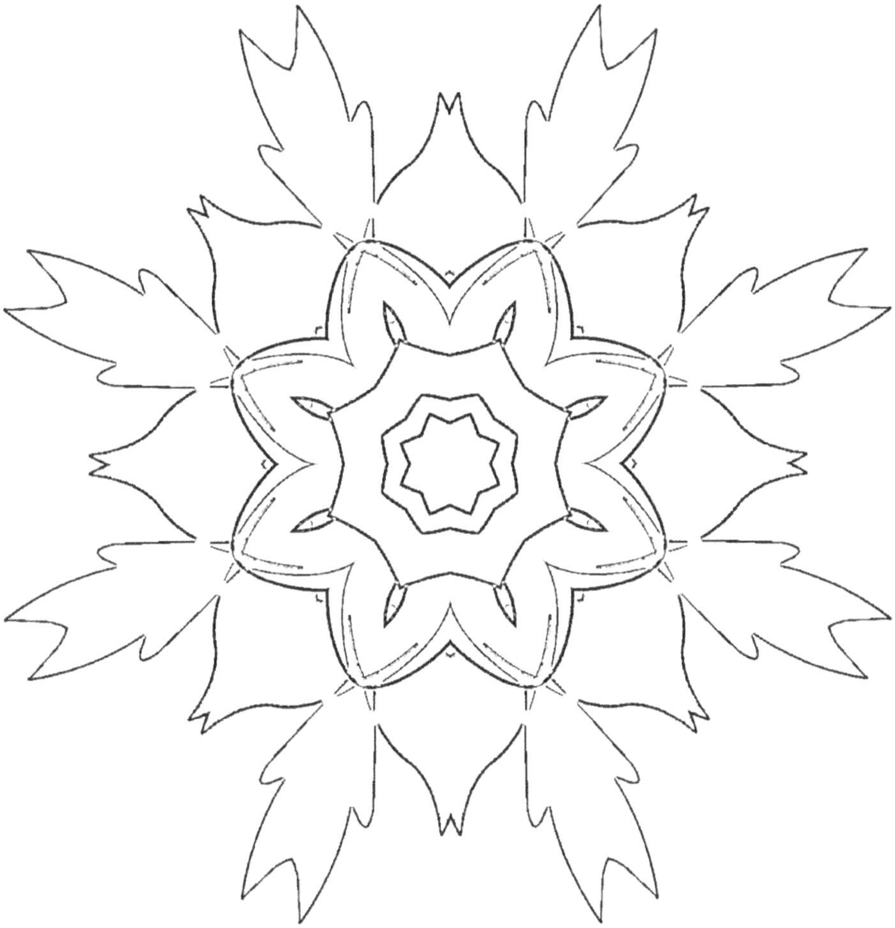

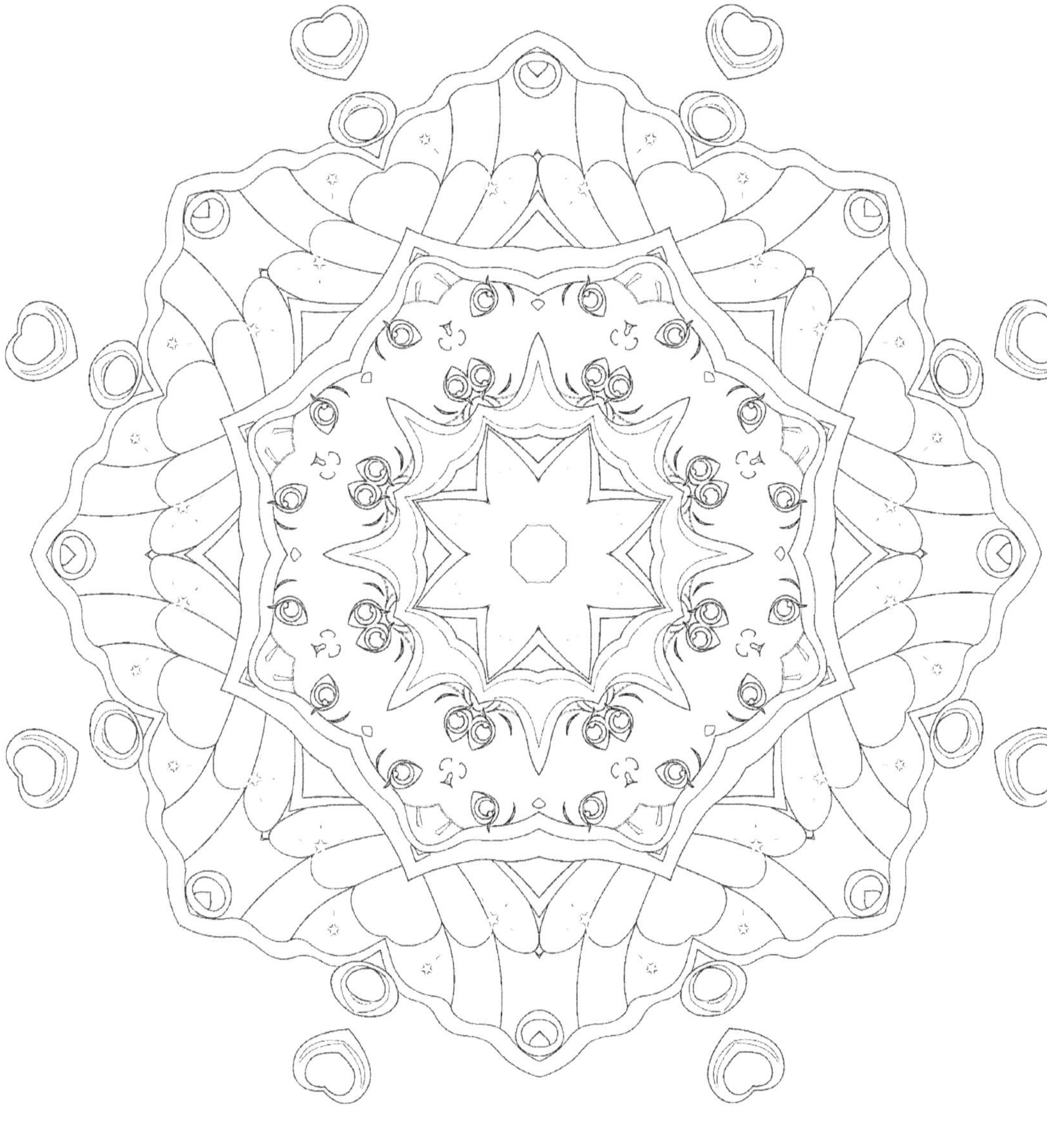

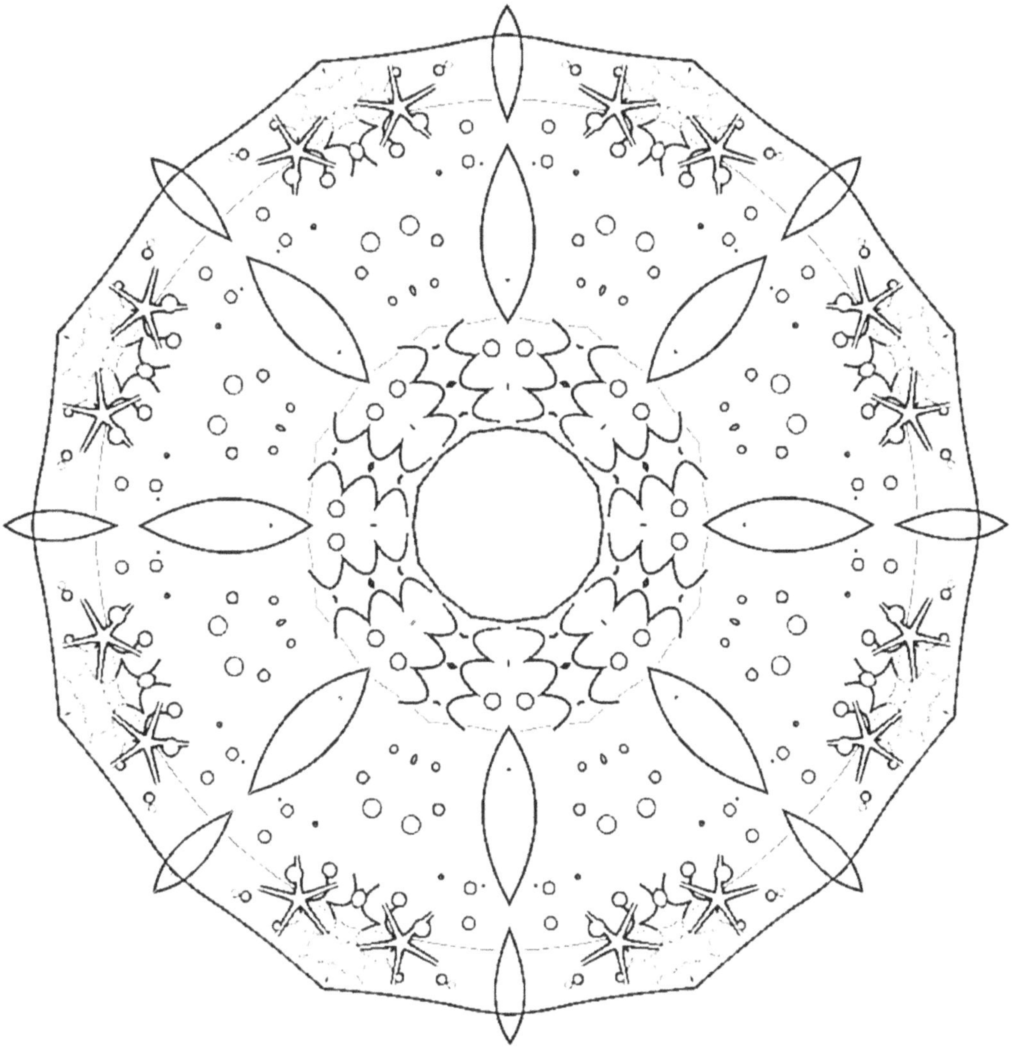

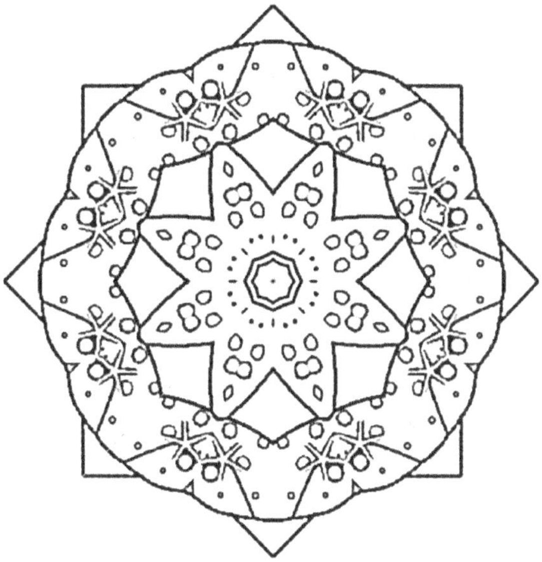

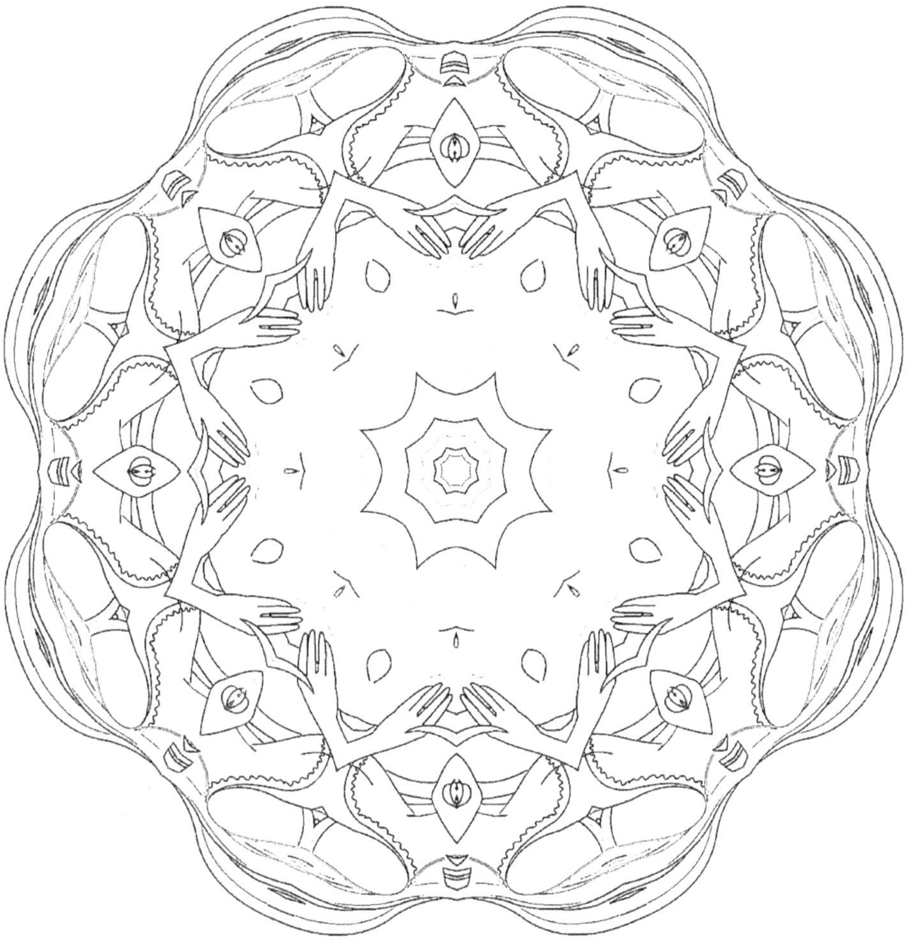

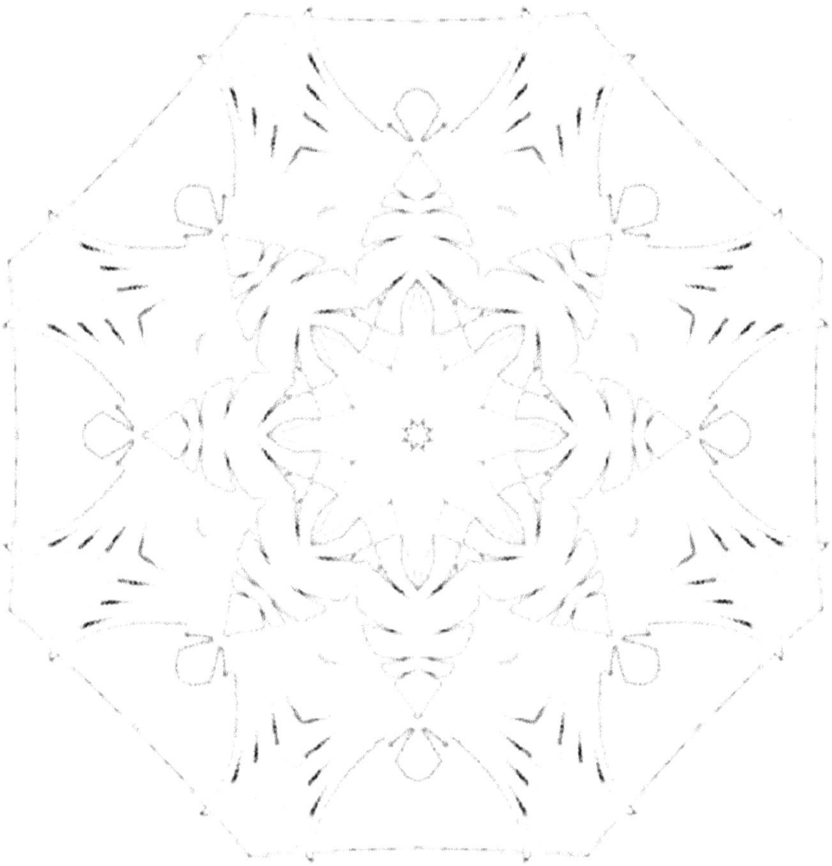

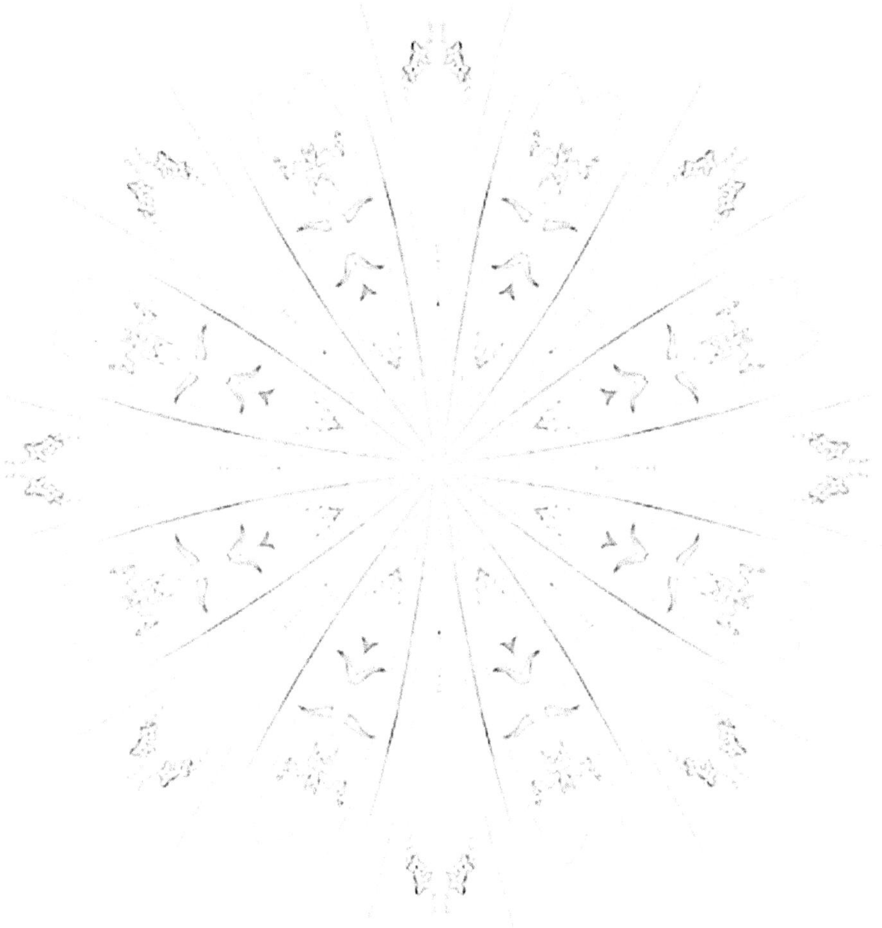

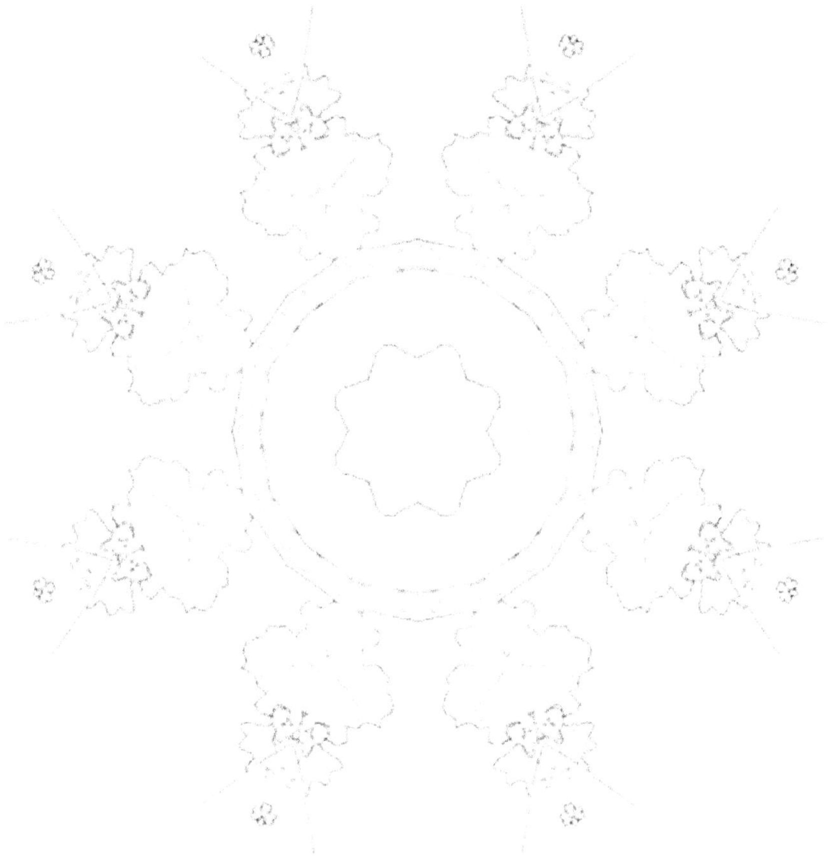

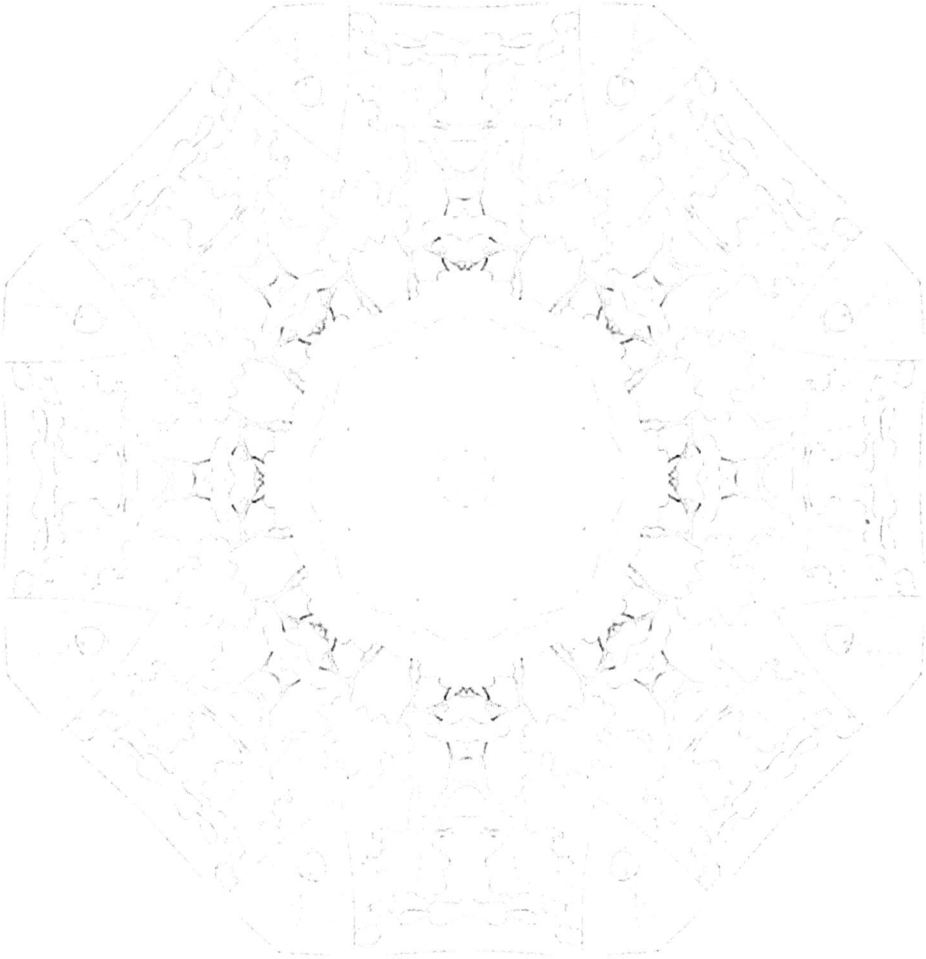

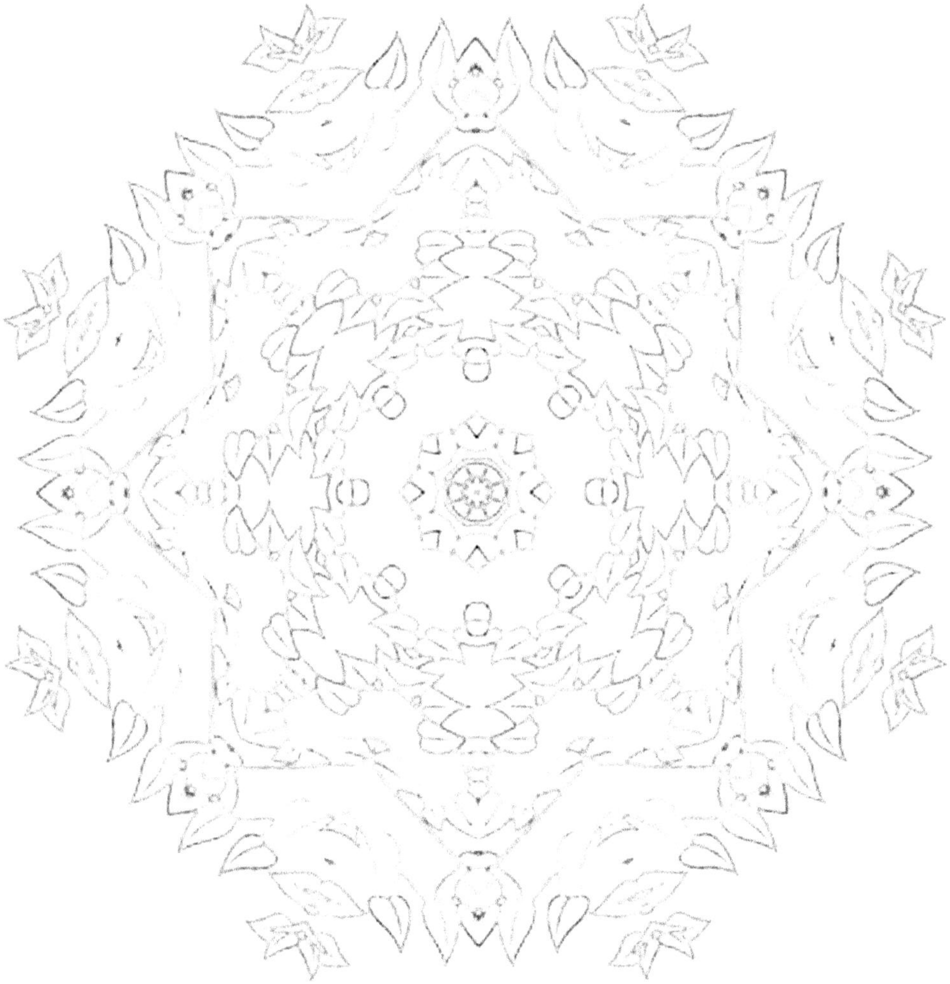

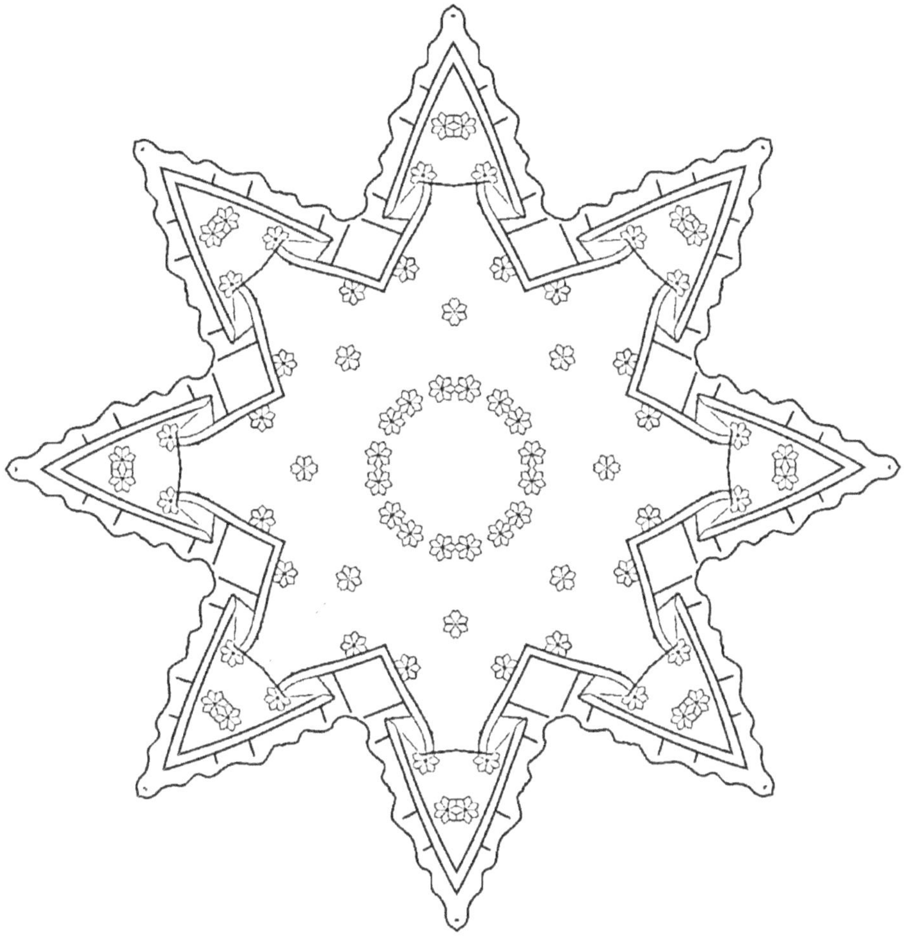

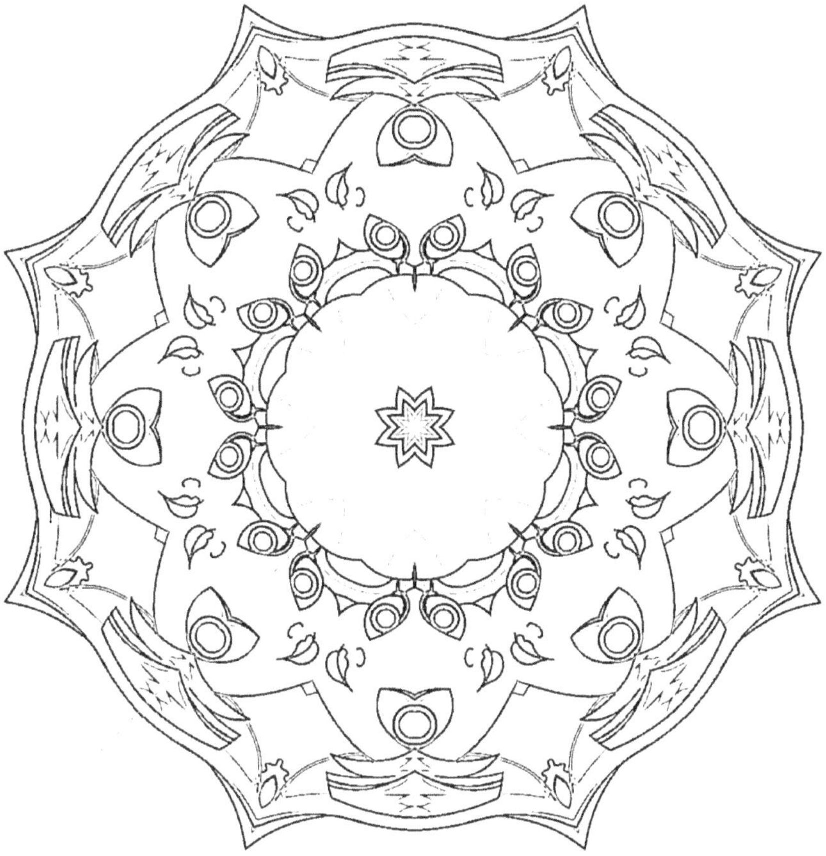

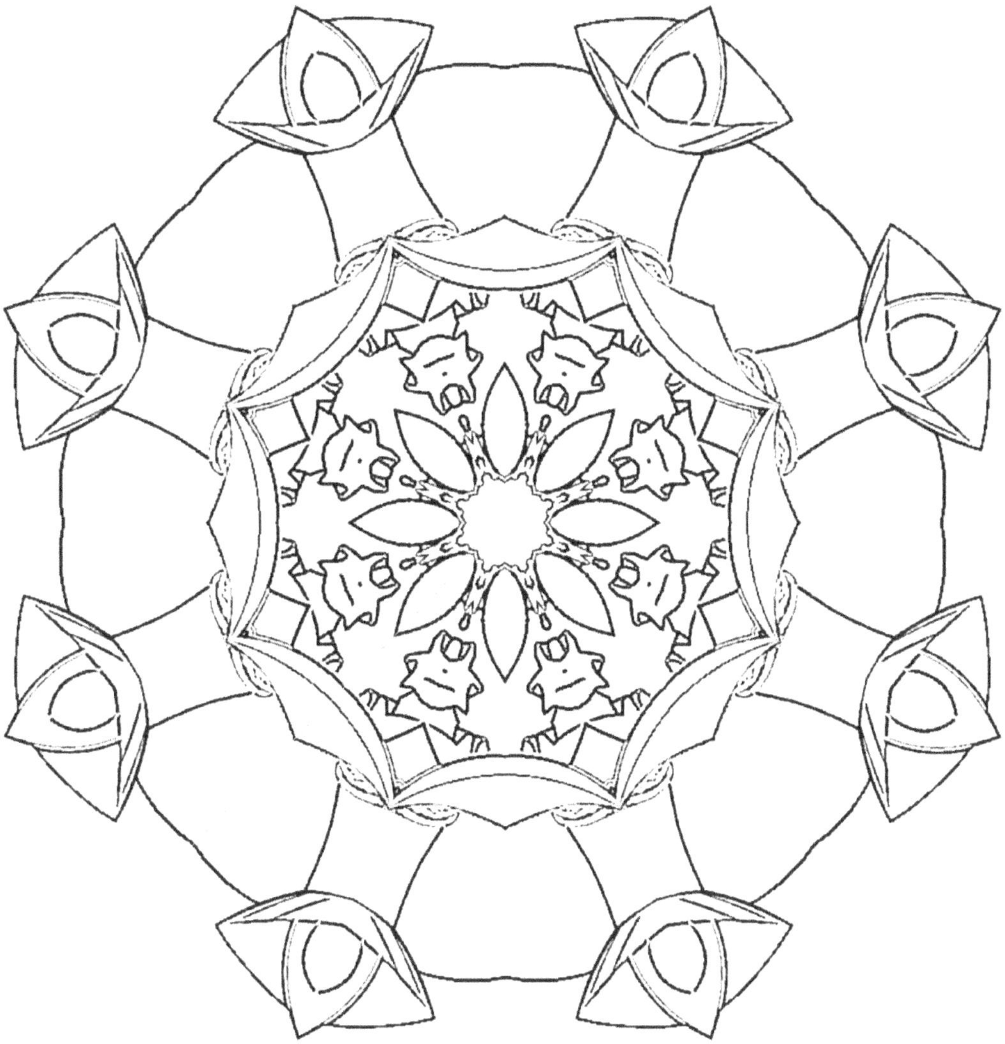

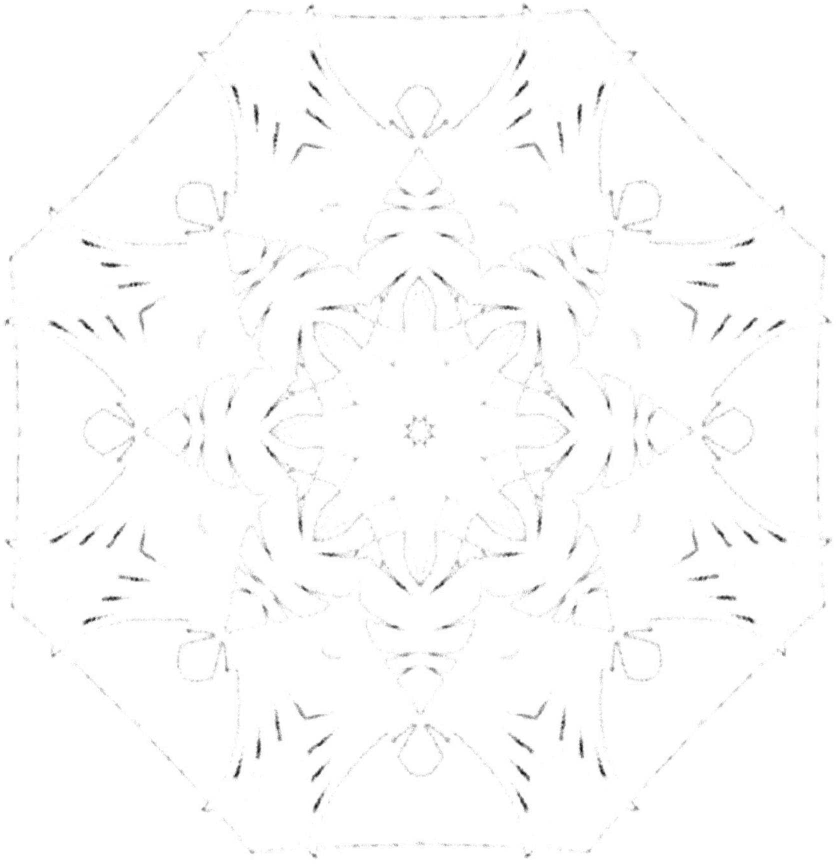

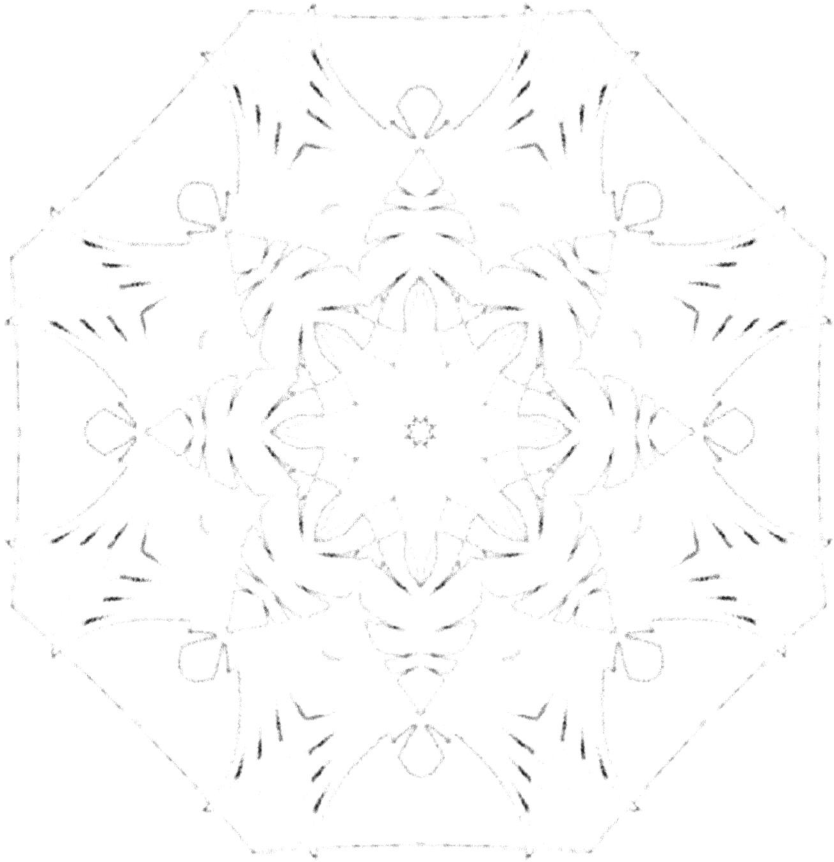

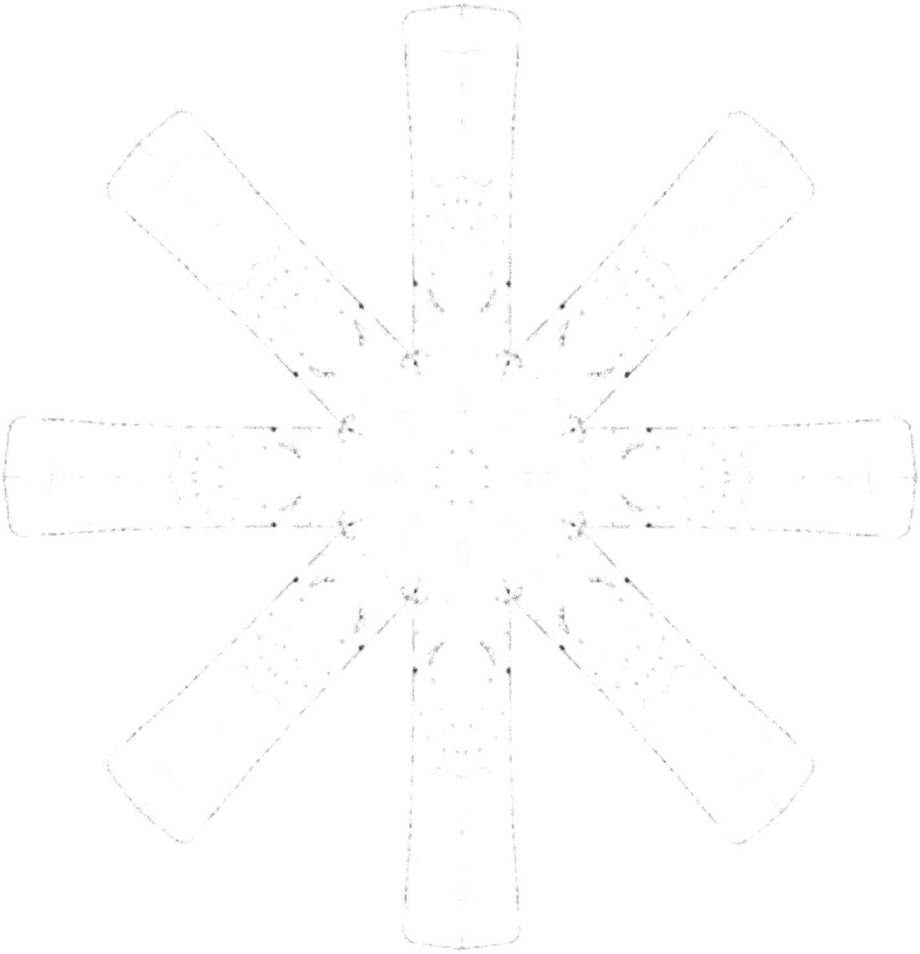

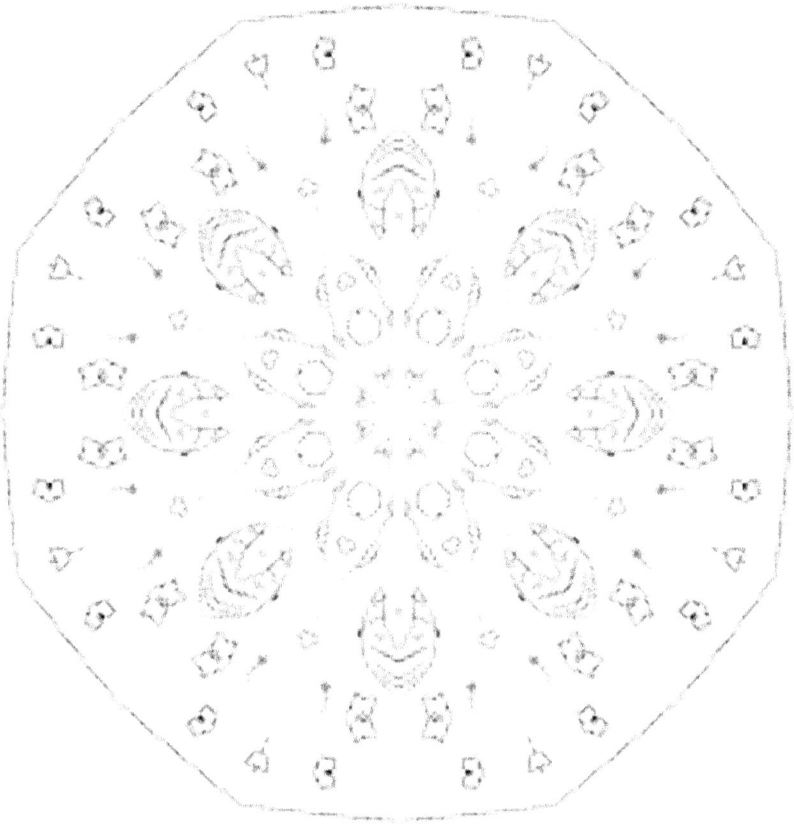

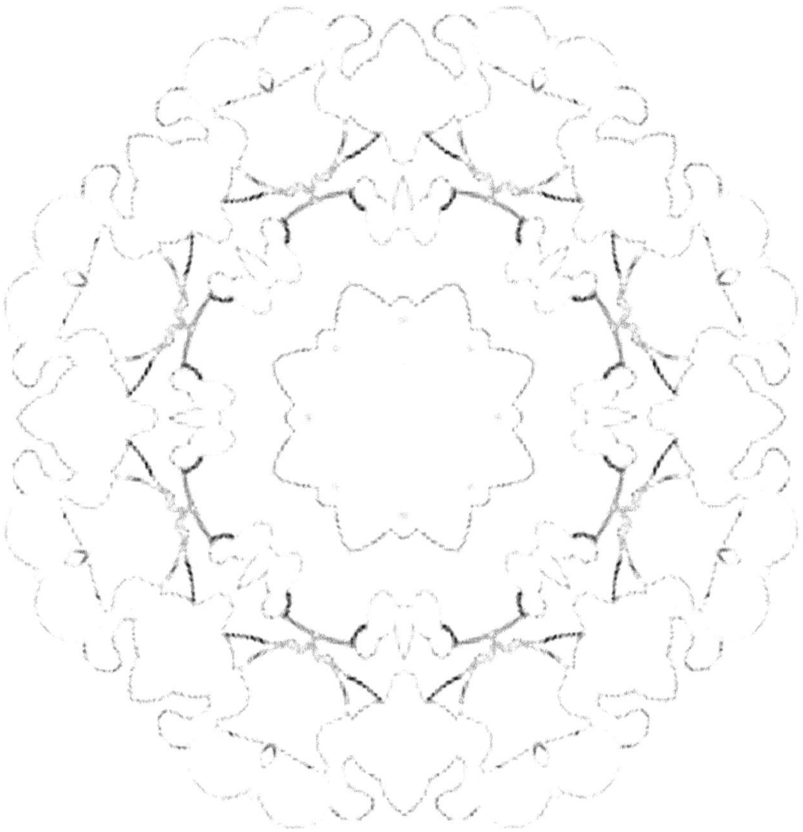

Note

www.ingramcontent.com/pod-product-compliance
Lightning Source LLC
Chambersburg PA
CBHW080649180526
45168CB00008B/3353
9781517441784